Spiritual Songs

MUSIC THAT BUILT A NATION

DR. NAIMA J. BUSH

WWW.WINSOR413.COM

Spiritual Songs Educational Curriculum
A Six Part Lesson Plan

The Creation and History of the Negro Spiritual
An Original American Musical Art Form

Dr. Naima Johnston Bush

* Teacher's Note – All lectures and lessons contain basic information on slavery and the slave trade that are important in regard to the creation of the Negro Spiritual as an original American art form. Please review all lesson plans beforehand and teach, modify and adapt the information that you believe is appropriate for your student's age range and educational development.

Spiritual Songs

Lesson One

Lesson One: Introduction of Spiritual Songs

Objective: To gain a basic understanding of the Mid Atlantic Slave Trade and an overview of the history of slavery in America.

Learning Outcomes

At the conclusion of this lesson students will:

- **Have a clear understanding of slavery and its impact on America**
- **Gain knowledge on Slave Castles, their locations and historical purpose**
- **Articulate the significance of The Door of No Return**
- **Utilize research skills in determining the number of slaves who perished on The Middle Passage while being able to define and describe The Middle Passage**
- **Demonstrate and be able to apply lesson vocabulary words that pertain to slavery and its origins in America**

Lesson One

Lecture: Slavery and Slave Castles

One of the evilest events in American history was the capture and theft of thousands of Africans from their homeland for over 245 years. Snared to fuel the building of North and South America, Africans from countries such as: Angola, Gambia and Senegal, were brought to the West African coast, chained and then kept for processing and impending departure in large buildings called Slave Castles. Slaves were captured by White Traders, and they were also traded to American and European Slave Catchers by other Africans as prisoners of war or in exchange for goods and supplies.

The Slave Castles were huge edifices that lined the coasts of West Africa and housed the chained stolen Africans in dark dungeons and cells as they unknowingly awaited their transport to North and South America and the Caribbean Islands. The first slaves landed in America in the 1620s and toiled on American soil until the end of the Civil War in 1865. For the purpose of this unit, we will be studying slavery only in the United States.

Today, several of these Slave Castles still stand, such as *The House of Slaves* located on Gorree Island in what is now Dakar, Senegal. *The House of Slaves* is currently a major museum dedicated to educating tourists to the horrors of the African slave trade.

Another Slave Castles that still stands is *El Amina Slave Castle*. For more information on *El Amina Slave Castle* view the video here:

https://www.youtube.com/watch?v=U7xO5IwJgZE or find the video by searching YouTube using the term, *El Amina Slave Castle.*

The Door of No Return

Thousands of people visit these Slave Castles each year to stand at what is called The Door of No Return and weep for what has been lost.

Before being loaded onto the slave ship to take what is now called The Middle Passage, slaves went through The Door of No Return, this was the doorway they passed through after they had been brought up from the dark dungeon of the Slave Castle and onto the beach for loading onto the slave ship that would take them to the Americas.

Once the Africans walked through this door, everything they knew and everyone they loved was forever gone. They left their language, culture, homeland and family behind on that bright African beach. They never returned, and their families never knew what happened to them. Slaves were taken to North and South America as well as the Caribbean Islands.

The Middle Passage

The Middle Passage is the actual name of the trip taken between Africa and the slave ship's final destination. The trip could take anywhere between three weeks and three months depending on the weather, the route the ship was taking, how many stops needed to be made during the voyage and various other factors. Slaves were loaded onto the ship in a way that would ensure maximum profit. Depending on the number of slaves being shipped, the size of the vessel and the greed of the slave ship captain, slaves would be loaded onto the boat either flat packed or tightly packed.

Flat packed meant that the slaves sailed across the Atlantic laying chained flat on their backs under the deck of the ship. Tightly packed meant that the slaves sailed across the Atlantic chained laying on their sides. Can you imagine making a three week to three-month trip flat on your back or on your side, chained in the dark? These were human beings packed tightly together unable to move, like books on a shelf. There was not enough space to sit up, there was no place to go to the bathroom, and the slaves were eating strange food and developed all kinds of sickness and disease.

They were brought up to the deck on occasion to exercise and be cleaned off with salt water that stung their sores and bruises. Many slaves died on the trip across the Atlantic and there are documented cases of crews throwing slaves overboard while they were still alive to save on supplies, to fix weight issues or, in later years, to try to avoid being pursued or caught by the British navy after the British outlawed slavery and often patrolled the African and Caribbean coastline.

Scholars disagree on the number of slaves that lost their lives during their time in the Slave Castles and on the Middle Passage. Some scholars estimate anywhere between two million and thirty million souls were lost in these tragic events.

Learning Exercise

Have the students Google this question, "How many Africans died during the Middle Passage?" Then have them create a chart listing all of the answers they find from the results comparing the various numbers.

They can also visit some of the websites they find and read more in depth information about the Slave Trade and Middle Passage. The teacher may want to do this exercise first and review the websites that come up to ensure they are academically appropriate for their students.

Learning Exercise
Questions to Ponder! Ask the students these questions at the close of the lecture:

Why do you think scholars have so many different numbers on how many slaves died making the trip across the Atlantic?

How many slaves do you think were taken from Africa? What do you think it was like making the trip from Africa to the Americas?

Learning Exercise
Geography Lessons

Pull up a map of Africa. What countries make up the Western part of the continent? What major cities are in these countries? What languages are spoken there and what cultural traditions do the people practices there? Who lives there? What is the weather like? What is the geography like? What is the history and current status of these nations today?

Ideas for Younger Learners

The lecture can be adapted for younger learners allowing the teacher to select which parts of history to emphasize. Young learners can be encouraged to do research on: animals native to the Western coast of Africa, what schools, music or dance are like in this region of the world or the various cultures and ethnic groups that live there.

Lecture Two – Conversion

We may never know the exact number of slaves who lost their lives during the Middle Passage. There was no technology to keep track of who was taken and who survived the journey. Also, many of the written records have been lost or destroyed, and since the slaves were not able to speak English when they arrived in America and were not asked their names, there is very little information available.

What we do know is that those who arrived on American shores were a people who were extremely strong and determined to live. Once the Africans made it to America they were no longer allowed to practice their African religions, they were forced to attend Christian church services and listen to sermons that often contradicted their lives as slaves.

They were told the stories of Exodus, where the great Biblical leader Moses led the Hebrew slaves out of bondage, into freedom and into a great land promised to them by God. The Africans heard scripture that stated that in Christ there was no slave and no master (Galatians 3 verse 28) and that in Heaven everyone would be equal. The stolen Africans embraced these stories that gave them hope and many converted and became Christians. This new faith birthed an original American art form known as the Negro Spiritual - songs of faith, hope, rebellion, sadness, instruction and victory.

Creative Vocabulary Exercises

Each lesson plan contains a list of vocabulary words and suggests three basic ways to use them. This handout gives the teacher additional vocabulary exercises to help the students define, apply and use these news words.

Connect Two
(Richek & McTague, 2008)
Write two lists of words on a blackboard or handout from the vocabulary words. Have students make connections between a word on the first list and a word on the second list, then have them explain the connections they made and why. This game assists in the development of critical thinking skills, abstract thinking and promotes interaction while introducing new concepts.

Dictionary Games
(Reiss, 2008)
Add more fun to defining words by setting up timed competitions. Pair or group students and allow them as a team to define the new words they are learning. This activity promotes basic research skills, motivates students and fosters student involvement.

Word Walls
(Gaquin, 2008)
Word walls can be used with any age learner. Create an eye-catching bulletin board and post new and interesting words on it in a format that can be easily removed (such as thumb tacks or double sided tape), added to or rearranged. As students learn new words, the old ones should be removed and saved for unit reviews, upcoming exams or projects. This exercise assists in content learning, reading skills and connections between new and old concepts.

Word Expert Cards
(Richek & McTague, 2008)
Have each student learn two or three of the new vocabulary words from the list then teach those words to the class or to a partner. Make the student a "word expert" and have them design a card for each vocabulary word using the actual definition, part of speech and an illustration. After a "word expert" is finished teaching their words to a peer, have them exchange cards with another student.

Lesson One Vocabulary Words and Terms

Instructions: These vocabulary words and phrases can be used in three ways:

1. Have students write down what they think the word means and then compare their definition with the dictionary's definition.
2. Conduct a spelling test or spelling bee or use other spelling games that help students identify and learn the proper spelling of these words.
3. Students can also be given an assignment to use each word in a sentence, essay, a poem or short story to assist in their development of language arts.

Conversion

Slavery

Slave Castles

The Door of No Return

The Middle Passage

Flat Packed

Tightly Packed

Negro Spirituals

Spiritual Songs

Lesson Two

Lesson Two: The Birth of the Negro Spiritual

Objective: To understand how the Negro Spiritual was created based on traditional African music and communication methods.

Learning Outcomes

At the conclusion of this lesson students will:

- Understand the importance of music in the daily lives of Africans
- Experience the significance of African Drums in communication
- Know how African music was reshaped to create the Negro Spiritual
- Explore poetry while engaging in creative writing skills
- Gain knowledge on vocabulary words that pertain to African music and other African cultural art forms

Lesson Two – Spiritual Songs

Lecture - The Heart Beat of Africa

Music was one of the most important parts of African cultural life. One of the primary instruments that Africans used and still use today is the drum. The drums were so important; they were used for religious services, celebrations, funerals and most importantly, they were used for communication. These are known as "The African Talking Drums."

Drum players in many West African villages were so skilled that they could "play" messages that could be heard and understood in distant villages. You could almost compare it to a modern day post office without the stamps or envelopes. The Talking Drums were used to spread and share all kinds of messages, and they were often used as a warning system. This warning system alerted other villages of danger in the area, such as coming tribal war, famine, sickness or even the arrival of slave catchers whose goal was to capture Africans and take them back to America as forced laborers.

After the Africans were captured and brought to America, they were no longer allowed to play the drums. The owners, who were called Masters, feared that the slaves would use the Talking Drums to speak to each other across plantations to plan uprisings and slave revolts.

The ability to communicate using the drums is called Drum Telegraphy – a system of communication used by Africans and other ethnic groups native to bush regions to transmit information and messages rapidly using intricate and highly developed drumming techniques.

What Kind of Drums Did They Play in West Africa?

The drum used was called the Djembe, pronounced as JEM-bay. Played with bare hands, the Djembe is shaped like a goblet and covered with animal skin secured by rope to the top of the drum.

Think About This!

"In Africa, New Guinea and the tropical America, people have used drum telegraphy to communicate with each other from far away for centuries. When European expeditions came into the jungles to explore the primeval forest, they were surprised to find that the message of their coming and their intention was carried through the woods a step in advance of their arrival. An African message can be transmitted at the speed of 100 miles in an hour."

From: Davis, Ernest (23 August 2011). "Information, from drums to Wikipedia". James Gleick. The Information: A History, A Theory, A Flood. 526pp. Fourth Estate. 978 0 00 722573 6. The Times Literary Supplement.

"Among the famous communication drums are the drums of West Africa (The Talking Drums). From regions known today as Nigeria and Ghana they spread across West Africa and to America and the Caribbean during the slave trade. There they were banned, because they were being used by the slaves to communicate over long distances in a code unknown to their enslavers."

Epstein, Dena J. (1963). "Slave Music in the United States Before 1860: A Survey of Sources (Part II)". Music Library Association Notes (Second Series) 20 (3): 377–390.

Learning Exercise
Questions to Ponder! Ask the students these questions at the close of the lecture:

Before coming to America, in what ways did the Africans use the drums?

What is Drum Telegraphy?

How much practice do you think it took to be able to play the African drums well enough so that they talked?

What did they call the drums they played in West Africa?

Why did the Masters forbid the slaves from playing drums on the plantations?

Learning Exercise
The Drums
Instructions: Read the poem, *The Drums* and answer the discussion questions.

The Drums

Rhythmic patterns
Match the beating
In the tasteless heat

Bodies pliable
Move in time to the vibrations
Writhing in the expressions of life

Beauty unforeseen
In agony that awaits
Messages transmitted on wind
Giving life to letters in the air

Words disguised
As thumping feet mask
Messages of warning

Celebrations of life and death
Worship of the One Who Is
Dancing as loud as spoken words
Players skillfully convey
That which needed to be known

The pounding fails, all is silent
At the wailing for the vanished

Gone across the big waters
Deaf to the music that speaks
Brutalized when found talking
In the ancient tongue

There are no drums
Across the sea

Dr. Naima Johnston Bush
© 2014 From the book, Psalms, Hymns and Spiritual Songs
All Rights Reserved

Learning Exercise
Poem Discussion Questions

**Instructions: Make copies of the poem *The Drums,* and pass them out to the
students. Have the students read the poem and circle any words they don't know
the meaning of. Once they have circled these words, have them define them and
share the meaning. Many of the words may be covered in the Vocabulary List
provided at the end of the lesson. Use the questions below as a guide for discussion,
as a writing assignment or as an advanced research project.**

What do you think the poem means?

What do you think the people are doing in the first part of the poem?

What message do you think is being played in the middle of the poem?

Who do you believe went across the big waters?

What do you think the ancient tongue is?

Why are there no drums across the sea?

Learning Exercise – Creative Writing

Instructions:

Now it's your turn! Write a poem about something that is important to you in life.
Imagine what it would be like if it was taken away. How would that make you feel? Try
to express those emotions in the poem you write. Think of interesting ways to say what
you want to say. This is a creative writing exercise so there is no right or wrong answer
just write the best poem you can in a way that makes sense to you.

Lecture Two – How Was the Negro Spiritual Created?

Since African Americans were no longer allowed to use the drums in everyday life they had to find new ways to express themselves musically. To celebrate, mourn, or occupy the time and most importantly in religious services, the slaves began to create their own songs that had no music. This is called A cappella singing – songs that are sung with no instruments.

Many Masters required their slaves to attend church services, but some did not. At first the Africans were unaccustomed to the church services which were quieter, had very little music and no dancing or loud expressions of faith through shouting.

In an effort to preserve their own faith traditions while also following their new faith, the slaves often snuck away into the corn fields and had special church meetings that allowed them to preach about freedom, to dance, shout and sing the new songs they created. These meetings were called Camp Meetings, and many African American churches in the southern part of the United States still have special church services called Camp Meetings today. Because the slaves snuck off into the corn fields to have these special church meetings, the first songs created by them were actually called Corn Ditties, because they were sung in the corn fields.

One of the most famous Corn Ditties is a song that many people still sing today. It's called, *Kum Ba Yah* or *Come by Here*. The song has two names, because no one is sure what the words really mean. Some believe that *Kum Ba Ya* is a mispronunciation of *Come by Here* made by struggling Africans trying to learn English. Some researchers believe it is a part of an unknown African language. The truth is we will never know, but what we do know is that this song calls upon God to look down upon his children and grant them some relief from their earthly pain and the suffering of slavery.

West African Sorrow Scale

As time passed Corn Ditties became known as Slaves Songs or Negro Spirituals. Almost all Negro Spirituals can be played on the piano using only the black piano keys. In music, this is called the Pentatonic Scale which has five notes per octave, but in Africa this scale was called something different, it was called the West African Sorrow Scale.

West Africans created their music using the Sorrow Scale. They brought this style of singing to America when they came and the scale became known musically as the slave scale. Negro Spirituals were created using the West African Sorrow Scale, songs such as *Swing Low Sweet Chariot, Every Time I Feel The Spirit* and even *Amazing Grace* can all be played using only the black keys on the piano.

Learning Exercise

Kum Ba Yah
Instructions: Listen to the song and have the students answer the questions below:

Go to the I-Tunes online store, and search for the song *Kum Ba Yah.* Listen to the various samples that are offered. How are the renditions the same? How are they different? Have you ever sung Kum Ba Yah? If so where and when? What do you think the song really means?

Kum Ba Yah

Kum ba ya my Lord, kum ba yah
Kum ba ya my Lord, kum ba yah
Kum ba ya my Lord, kum ba yah
Oh Lord, kum ba yah

Someone's singing Lord, kum ba yah
Someone's singing Lord, kum ba yah
Someone's singing Lord, kum ba yah
Oh Lord, kum bay yah

Someone's crying, Lord, kum ba yah
Someone's crying, Lord, kum ba yah
Someone's crying, Lord, kum ba yah
Oh Lord, kum ba yah

Someone's praying, Lord, kum ba yah
Someone's praying, Lord, kum ba yah
Someone's praying, Lord, kum ba yah
Oh Lord, kum ba ya

Lesson Two Vocabulary Words and Terms

Instructions: These vocabulary words and phrases can be used in three ways.

1. Have students write down what they think the word means and then compare their definition with the dictionary's definition.
2. Conduct a spelling test or spelling bee or use other spelling games that help students identify and learn the proper spelling of these words.
3. Students can also be given an assignment to use each word in a sentence, essay, a poem or short story to assist in their development of language arts.

A cappella

Banned

Communication

Convey

Expedition

Goblet

Intricate

Pliable

Telegraphy

Transmitted

Vibrations

Writhing

Learning Exercise

Quick Quiz
Instructions: Answer the following questions from Lesson Two to the best of your ability.

1. **What is a Corn Ditty?**

2. **What is a Camp Meeting?**

3. **What is the West African Sorrow Scale?**

4. **What keys are used in the West African Sorrow Scale?**

5. **What Does Kum Ba Yah mean?**

Learning Exercises

Ideas for Younger Learners on Lessons One and Two:

1. Have the students do an online search using the key words, Talking Drum Videos. There are several on YouTube that will give the students excellent visual aid examples of this unique way of communication. Have the students write down the details from the videos that they find most interesting or is new information for them and have them share this information in a class presentation or written essay.

2. Take the students to a performance of African Dance, search for African Dance videos on YouTube or take an African Dance class in your area by locating a class via Google, Craig's List or contact your local Cultural Arts Centers.

3. Visit the library and find African drum music and picture books on African cultural life.

4. Make your own African Drum. The resource section of this manual has a website link that contains instructions for creating your own African Drum. Instructions to create drums range from easy to more the advanced.

5. Create Your Own Drum Language. Have your students create simple rhythm patterns using drums they made, hand claps or even beating on the table. For example, they could create patterns to express sadness, one to express danger/warning, one to express happiness/peace, and one to express celebration/excitement. They could even create patterns that mean specific phrases or words of their choice.

6. Kum Ba Yah is a very easy song to learn. If you know it, teach it to the students and have them sing the song at the end of each lesson.

7. Have the students create art pieces of drums using paint, mosaic tiles, ink, pastels, clay or crayons.

Spiritual Songs

Lesson Three

Lesson Three: The Different Uses of the Negro Spiritual

Objective: To gain a basic understanding of the different uses of the Negro Spiritual during slavery in daily life.

Learning Outcomes

At the conclusion of this lesson students will:

- Have a clear understanding of the different uses of the Negro Spiritual in daily life
- Gain a basic knowledge of slavery as an economic institution
- Identify and articulate Call and Response Singing and the use of it in modern music and society
- Utilize research and writing skills to explore various aspects of slavery, African American music and slavery's impact on slave families
- Gain knowledge on vocabulary words that pertain to various aspects of slavery and the Negro Spiritual

Lesson Three – Spiritual Songs

Lecture – Introduction

The original use of the Negro Spiritual was to express in song the new faith the Africans, who were now known as Negros, had come to believe in. But as time passed, the songs became much more then songs of faith. The Spiritual was used not only in church services as songs of praise and worship, but they were also used to express the loss of family, to coordinate work efforts, to lead escaped slaves to freedom and to shout out in rebellion against the injustices of human bondage.

Here is a brief list of Negro Spirituals used in many church services, cultural celebrations and even in rallies and political meetings that were held to change policies and unjust laws in America:

- *Nobody Knows The Trouble I've Seen*
- *Every Time I Feel The Spirit*
- *Ezekiel Saw The Wheel*
- *Ani't No Grave Gonna Hold My Body Down*
- *Amen*
- *Michael Row The Boat Ashore*
- *We Shall Overcome*
- *When The Saints Go Marching In*

For an exhaustive list of songs that are Negro Spirituals visit www.negrospirituals.com and review the songs listed there.

Learning Exercise
Questions to Ponder! Ask your students these questions at the close of the lecture:

Review the list of Negro Spirituals online. When looking at the list, did you find any songs that you knew?

Do you remember where you learned these songs or where you sung them?

Are you surprised at some of the songs you found listed?

If you did not find any songs you know, visit the library to check out a CD on Negro Spirituals, visit the I-Tunes Store and download one of the songs listed above or search YouTube or Spotify to see if you can find a recording of one of these songs.

Learning Exercise
For Younger Learners

Have the students sing the Negro Spirituals that they know or teach them one.

Teacher's Note: (Negro Spirituals that many people know include: *This Little Light of Mine, Swing Low Sweet Chariot, Give Me That Old Time Religion.* **These songs are usually sung in scouting groups, youth groups, church services and can sometimes be found in modern media.)**

Lecture Two – Negro Spiritual in Every Day Life

Long before TV, video games, MP3 players and the internet, there were very few choices for entertainment. There were laws in place prohibiting slaves from learning to read and write, so they could not pass the time reading. There were also many laws that prohibited gatherings of slaves and restricting their travel, so there were very few gatherings of various groups of slaves unless special permission could be obtained from their Masters.

Slaves spent a good deal of time (after their work was done for the day) sitting together with other slaves on their plantations, talking, telling stories, passing along news that they had overheard in the Master's house or from slaves who could travel (such as the slave who drove the Master's wagon) and singing.

The Negro Spirituals developed into creative expressions of stories, jokes, life and happenings around the plantation. Here's an example:

Scandalize My Name - Paul Roberson - https://youtu.be/z0X0uw9RzUo

Remember!

Slaves could not come and go as they pleased. They could never sleep in, or choose what they ate or were they went. When slaves had children, their children were also slaves, so every baby born became the property of the Master.

Webster's Definition of Property

Something owned or possessed, such as a piece of real estate

The exclusive right to possess, enjoy, and dispose of a thing

Ownership, something to which a person or business has a legal title

Because slaves were not seen as humans but as property, they could be killed, beaten, brutalized, bought and sold whenever the Master decided to. Slaves were sold for many reasons including: economic hardship, to settle debt, death of owners, as punishment or sometimes for no reason at all. As property, a slave owner could name his slaves in his will so that other family members could inherit them. Slaves could be given as gifts from one member of the family to another. The number of slaves owned by a family often determined the amount of wealth a family had. The more slaves you owned, the more money you had.

Imagine what it would be like if you were a child, and someone took you away from home and sold you far away from your family. The majority of slaves that were sold never saw their loved ones again, and those remaining were not given any information about where their loved ones were taken.

The separation of families was a constant source of fear and left lasting anguish in many lives. Songs such as, *Sometimes I Feel Like A Motherless Child,* were born from this unbearable pain. Yet the slaves did survive and kept going with hope in their hearts that one day they would be free and find their loved ones again.

Learning Exercise
Personal Reflection Essay Instructions:

Have the students write a personal essay or journal entry on the question, "What would it be like to be sold away from your family and friends?" Creative writing should be encouraged and students should write an essay that truly expresses their thoughts and feelings on what it would be like to be a slave and what it would mean to be sold away from family. Teachers should gauge if this exercise is appropriate for their students based on their emotional, personal and spiritual well being.

Lecture Three – Call and Response Singing

One of the greatest uses of the Negro Spiritual by the slaves was to coordinate work in the field such as picking cotton or planting corn. The songs were also used for completing large tasks such as laying road or moving objects. Finally, the songs were used for communication between the slaves as they worked together to complete their tasks.

These types of songs are defined as Call and Response Songs or Call and Response Singing. One person is assigned as the leader of the song, or the "Caller." Others in the group, or the workers, are defined as the "Responders."

The leader or Caller sings a phrase which contains a specific direction or action for the workers to complete. For example, the leader might call out, "We're gonna pick two bales, two bales pick!" The Responders or workers would then respond with an answer and an action, something like, "2 bales pick, 2 bales picked!" In this way, the slaves worked together to achieve their grueling workload.

Call and Response Singing was also used in church services. The Caller would give a command about what the congregation needed to do to represent their Christian faith, and the responders would respond with the action they were going to take. An example of this would be songs such as: *This Little Light of Mine* and *Scandalize My Name* which is mentioned in the previous section.

Call and Response singing has always been an important part of African American cultural heritage. From the shores of Africa, to the music of the 1930's, to illustrations in movies and expanding to Hip Hop and modern R and B today. Call and Response can even be found in cheerleading chants, Rock and Roll music and instrumental songs, where the various instruments do the calling and responding.

Learning Exercise
For an in-depth study of Call and Response singing, review the following videos listed below:

Call and Response Videos:

Coordinating Big Tasks:
The Color Purple Work Song - https://www.youtube.com/watch?v=H8wYEAjOumU

African Call and Response
Call and Response in Africa - https://youtu.be/QFWRcXYsYMo

Popular Call and Response, The Early Years
Cab Calloway – Sesame Street Version - https://youtu.be/esnDnIK2v1g
Cab Calloway 1934 Audio Original - https://youtu.be/jDK7sRLn-3E

Call and Response in Opera - https://youtu.be/S6EOXT6_inw

Hip Hop and R and B
Beyoncé's Call and Response - https://youtu.be/VBmMU_iwe6U

Cheerleading Call and Response - https://youtu.be/_WgNlD5Brw0

Learning Exercise
Call and Response In Modern Music

Have the students listen to Beyoncé's song, *Girls*, if it is deemed appropriate for the educational community. Have the students identify the Call and the Response in the song.

Spiritual Songs Curriculum
Dr. Naima Johnston Bush © 2017

Answer: The call is the actual question, "Who runs the world?" The response is the actual answer, "Girls!"

After viewing the various Call and Response videos, have the students create their own Call and Response Song using modern issues and concerns. Make sure they decide what the topic of the song will be before creating it. Students can be encouraged to create a song to coordinate a work task or a faith song, or even a song to pass the time.

Learning Exercise
Possible Research Projects:

Have your students write a research paper on one of the following research topics. In order to challenge as well as meet the needs of each student, each teacher should determine the number of pages and number and types of sources that should be used for the project. Creative projects, such as raps, poetry, diagrams, interviews or art projects should also be encouraged and considered.

Possible Research Projects/Topics for Older Learners:

Economic Conditions in The South During Slavery

Paul Roberson: The Man and His Music

The Negro Spiritual and Opera Music

Civil Rights and The Negro Spiritual

Lesson Three Vocabulary Words and Terms

Instructions: These vocabulary words can be used in three ways.

1. Have students write down what they think the word means and then compare their definition with the dictionary's definition.
2. Conduct a spelling test or spelling bee or use other spelling games that help students identify and learn the proper spelling of these words.
3. Students can also be given an assignment to use each word in a sentence, essay, a poem or short story to assist in their development of language arts.

Bondage

Economics

Exclusive

Exhaustive

Faith

Property

Rebellion

Response

Scandalize

Learning Activity

Quick Quiz
Instructions: Answer the following questions from Lesson Three to the best of your ability.

How was the Negro Spiritual used in daily life?

In your own words describe, Call and Response Singing:

How Is Call and Response used today in music?

If you were a slave you were considered property, what did that mean?

Spiritual Songs

Lesson Four

Lesson Four: Escape and Freedom

Objective: To gain a basic understanding of methods the slaves used to escape bondage, hide directions in Negro Spiritual Songs and the Underground Railroad.

Learning Outcomes

At the conclusion of this lesson students will:

- Have a clear understanding of various methods slaves used for escape
- Define and describe Code Songs
- Articulate the significance of songs such as, *Follow The Drinking Gourd*
- Develop research skills to explore subjects such as Astronomy and Geography
- Utilize vocabulary words that pertain to slavery, escape and freedom

Lesson Four

Lecture – Running For Freedom

Many slaves attempted to run away from their Masters to find freedom in the Northern states of America, Canada and even Mexico and Africa. Many were successful in their search for freedom using a systemic network of houses, churches and other plantations to escape from bondage. This was called the Underground Railroad and those individuals committed to assisting the slaves to freedom were called Conductors. The Underground Railroad was not an actual railroad, rather slaves were moved along the route to freedom by many White men, women and free Blacks, who hated slavery and wanted to see an end to this cruel institution.

It is estimated that over 100,000 slaves escaped from slavery between 1800 and 1865.

To assist the slaves in escape, many Negro Spirituals were created to give direction on methods that could be used to find their way North. Songs contained hidden maps, instructions on how to evade slave catchers and code words that could be sung to identify those dedicated to assisting the slaves in finding their freedom. Slaves also used quilts to hide maps and directions for escape as well.

Several Negro Spirituals describe crossing over the River Jordan which is a prominent river in biblical stories. Jordan is actually a metaphor in the Negro Spiritual Songs.

Webster's Definition of Metaphor

A word or phrase for one thing that is used to refer to another thing in order to show or suggest that they are similar

An object, activity, or idea that is used as a symbol of something else

For example, your head is as hard as a rock or the bed was as cold as ice.

In the Negro Spiritual, crossing over the River Jordan is a metaphor for crossing the Ohio River, which separated Kentucky in the South from Ohio in the North. If slaves could cross this river, they were often safe and able to continue further North assuring their freedom. A great many slaves did settle down in parts of Ohio, Indiana and Michigan.

Songs that mention places such as Heaven, Zion and Paradise are often code words for places like Ohio, Canada and Liberia in West Africa.

The Negro Spiritual song, *Wade In The Water*, is actually an instructional song. Every human being has a unique smell, and dogs can smell so well, that they can be trained to locate the scent of individual people. Because of their great ability to smell, dogs were used to track and pick up the scent of the runaway slaves. Dogs, however, cannot smell through water, because the water washes away the scent and confuses the animals. If slaves could find water, a river, or creek, and could get into the water, their scent was hidden from the dogs. *Wade in the Water* was a song used to instruct slaves on how to confuse the dogs and evade capture.

The Ohio River

Historically, the Ohio River has been one of the dividing lines between the Southern United States and the Northern States. Many slaves crossed the Ohio River to gain their freedom and made their homes in Cincinnati, one of the largest cities on the Northern side of the Ohio River during slavery. Today, on the banks of the mighty Ohio, there sits a museum dedicated to educating the nation about slavery, both historically and in modern times. The museum is called, *The Freedom Center,* is a must-see if you are ever in the Cincinnati, Ohio area.

Learning Exercises
Ohio River Geography Project

Have the students conduct a research project on The Ohio River. Students can be encouraged to focus on one general aspect of the river such as trade over the last 100 years, famous river crossings by slaves, or give a general overview. Here are some general questions to guide their inquiry:

How many states does The Ohio River run through?

Answer: ***At least six, and borders at least fifteen.***

Where does it begin, end and how long is it?

Answer: ***Pittsburgh, PA to Cairo, IL, 981 Miles***

What cities sit on its banks and which cities are the largest?

Answer: Pittsburgh is the largest, Cincinnati the second largest. Other cities include: Wheeling, WV and Louisville, KY.

Review maps to understand how the river flows and where it goes.

Answer: The Ohio River runs into the Mississippi and has tributaries such as, the Tennessee River, the Hocking River, the Scioto River and many others.

What types of fish live in the river, and what types of animals live and depend on its waters?

Answer: Bass, Bowfin, Carp, Catfish, Gar, Perch, Pike and Walleye to name a few – over 100 species of fish live in the river. There is an excellent episode of Animal Planet's River Monsters on the Gar Fish. Animals include: fox, deer, muskrats, raccoons, fresh water mussels, mink and migratory birds.

Other Questions for Consideration:

What types of trade has occurred over the years on the river?

What types of dams have been built along the river and what purpose do they serve?

What other names has the Ohio River had?

Who is credited with discovering the river and who originally lived on its banks?

What other interesting facts can the students find? Example: The Ohio River serves as the primary drinking source for over 3 million people.

Study of Faith – The Ohio and The Jordan. Have the students compare and contrast the historical River Jordan as described in the Bible and other texts with the geography of the Ohio River, asking similar questions about wild life, climate, length, etc.

Learning Exercise
Ohio River Geography Project

The Ohio River has played a great role in slavery and freedom. Conduct a brief research project on the history, uses and geography of the river. Here are some general questions to guide your research project:

How many states does The Ohio River run through?

Where does it begin, end and how long is it?

What cities sit on its banks and which cities are the largest?

Review maps of Ohio to understand how the river flows and what other states the river runs through.

What types of fish live in the river and what types of animals live and depend on its waters?

What types of trade has occurred over the years on the river?

What types of dams have been built along the river and what purpose do they serve?

What other names has the Ohio River had?

Who is credited with discovering the river and who originally lived on its banks?

What other interesting facts can the students find? Example: The Ohio River serves as the primary drinking source for over 3 million people.

Lecture Two – Conductors of the Underground Railroad

Harriet Tubman, an escaped slave is one of the most famous Conductors of the Underground Railroad. She returned to the South several times, with a pistol, to assist slaves in their flight for freedom. But Harriet Tubman was more than just a Conductor of the Underground Railroad. Harriet served as a spy for the Union Army, a nurse, an advocate and activist for free slaves.

There were many other Conductors of the Underground Railroad, of both African and European descent that did great works to end slavery and to assist in their flight to freedom. Have the students use Google or some other search engine to discover these unsung heroes. Have them start by using the search term, Conductors of the Underground Railroad and have them share the stories they have read about and learned with others.

Field Trips

Students should be taken or encouraged to visit the library, speak with the research or reference librarian to discover new ways to use the library and its resources to conduct research and educational projects. If near Cincinnati, Ohio a trip to the Freedom Center makes a great field trip. http://www.freedomcenter.org/

There are many other museums and organizations that you can take your students to visit as well. Listed below are a few ideas, but there are African American Historical Societies, living history museums and other plantations not listed below that can be visited by doing a search for such organizations or places by state.

Carnton Plantation or The Hermitage
Nashville, TN

Kingsley Plantation
Jacksonville, FL

Schomberg Library and Museum
Harlem, New York

Civil Rights Museum
Memphis, TN

African American History Museum
Wilberforce, Ohio

Smithsonian Museum on African American History and Culture
Washington, DC

Learning Exercise
Another Option

Another great project would be to study the use of quilts as maps for the Underground Railroad and as a method of escape.

Learning Exercise
Modern Slavery

Most people forget that slavery still exists today. If you have older students, you can have them do a research project on the various types of slavery that is occurring today, how people are becoming slaves, and how they can help combat it. One of the most prominent issues is Sex Trafficking and although a very intense and disturbing crime, if the students are old enough to understand and grasp its implications they should be educated on the issues.

Have the students compare and contrast modern slavery with pre Civil War Slavery. How are they similar? How are they different? How can they get in involved and become "Virtual Conductors" to help bring an end to this issue? Furthermore, how can students protect themselves from becoming victims of such a crime.

Have the students plan an awareness event, do a fundraiser for a reputable group or volunteer at an event to end Human Trafficking and Modern Day Slavery.

For More Information Visit:

https://traffickingresourcecenter.org/

https://en.wikipedia.org/wiki/List_of_organizations_that_combat_human_trafficking

Lecture Three – Follow The Drinking Gourd, A Code Song Lesson

Follow The Drinking Gourd, is a Negro Spiritual that is believed to have been used as a secret message song that offered the slaves clues to escape hidden in the lyrics. These clues were actually directions to lead fugitive slaves from the South to the free states of the North and to Canada.

According to legend, the song was created and used by a Conductor of the Underground Railroad named Peg Leg Joe. Peg Leg Joe was a white abolitionist with one leg, who traveled amongst the various Southern plantations disguised as a laborer, teaching the song and disseminating the secrets of escape. *Follow the Drinking Gourd* is one of the few surviving examples of the secret songs and codes hidden in the fascinating history of the Negro Spiritual.

What Is A Gourd?

A gourd is a fleshy, typically large fruit with a hard skin, like a pumpkin or a squash. It was often dried and hallowed out by Africans and African Americans and used to dip into barrels or buckets as a cup for drinking water.

The Drinking Gourd actually refers to the star constellation of The Big Dipper. The Big Dipper when followed points directly to Polaris, the star in the sky most close to True North. It is also the tip of the handle in the constellation of the Little Dipper. By following the gourd in the sky, the slaves could navigate their way north and onward to freedom.

Over the last decade, some scholars have refuted the authenticity of the song. Some believe that it is simply a tale of slavery folklore and that there was no Peg Leg Joe or route on the Underground Railroad that used the Big Dipper as its guide. The truth is we can never know for certain as there are no real historical records on the subject. But the song itself makes a compelling case that there is some truth in the reason for the creation and hidden clues in the song.

Lesson Four Vocabulary Words and Terms

Instructions: These vocabulary words can be used in three ways.

1. Have students write down what they think the word means and then compare their definition with the dictionary's definition.
2. Conduct a spelling test or spelling bee or use other spelling games that help students identify and learn the proper spelling of these words.
3. Students can also be given an assignment to use each word in a sentence, essay, a poem or short story to assist in their development of language arts.

Abolitionist

Authenticity

Compelling

Conductor

Constellation

Creation

Disseminating

Escape

Folklore

Gourd

Legend

Lyrics

Metaphor

Network

Quail

Scent

Systematic

Learning Exercise
Follow The Drinking Gourd

The original lyrics to *Follow The Drinking Gourd* were sung using improper English as the slaves had no education and were not taught to speak correctly or to read. Below are the original lyrics to the song as the slaves would have sung them. The second set of lyrics was written in modern English so that the students can understand the actual words to the song.

Questions to Ponder!
Ask the students these questions at the close of the lecture:

Try to read the lyrics as they were originally written without looking at the modern lyrics. What do you think the lyrics mean? How hard is it to speak and/or read these lyrics? What parts of the song give specific directions? How is Peg Leg Joe mentioned in the song? How hard do you think it would have been to follow the map hidden in the song?

Now look at the modern lyrics. Do you better understand the song? What became clear that wasn't clear before? Based on your reading, do you think the song is really a map or just folklore? Why or Why not?

Follow The Drinking Gourd
Original Song Lyrics

VERSE 1
When the sun come back,
When the firs' quail call,
Then the time is come
Foller the drinkin' gou'd.

CHORUS
Foller the drinkin' gou'd,
Foller the drinkin' gou'd;
For the ole man say,
"Foller the drinkin' gou'd."

VERSE 2
The riva's bank am a very good road,
The dead trees show the way,
Lef' foot, peg foot goin' on,
Foller the drinkin' gou'd.

VERSE 3
The riva ends a-tween two hills,
Foller the drinkin' gou'd;
'Nuther riva on the other side
Foller the drinkin' gou'd.

VERSE 4
Wha the little riva
Meet the grea' big un,
The ole man waits--
Foller the drinkin' gou'd.

Modern Song Lyrics

VERSE 1
When the sun comes back,
and the first quail calls,
Follow the drinking gourd
The old man is awaiting for to carry you to freedom
If you follow the drinking gourd.

CHORUS

Follow the drinking gourd,
Follow the drinking gourd,
For the old man is awaiting for to carry you to freedom
If you follow the drinking gourd.

VERSE 2
The river bank will make a mighty good road
The dead trees show you the way
Left foot, peg foot, traveling on
Follow the drinking gourd.

VERSE 3
The river ends between two hills,
Follow the drinking gourd,
There's another river on the other side,
Follow the drinking gourd.

VERSE 4
Where the great big river meets the little river
Follow the drinking gourd
The old man is awaiting for to carry you to freedom
If you follow the drinking gourd.

Learning Exercises for Younger Learners on Lesson Four:

Have the students conduct an online search and find images of gourds, have them answer the following questions:

What types of fruit or vegetables are defined as gourds?

After examining the images ask the students, if there are any gourds in their homes now? Are there any that your family eats or have eaten?

Take the student to the supermarket to purchase a gourd. Have them slice it in half, remove the seeds and allow the gourd to dry on newspaper. Can you use it as a drinking gourd?

What other possible uses could a gourd have in every day life?

Video Exercises

There are many interesting videos on YouTube to guide the students in making a drinking gourd and other gourd uses.

This website has an excellent blog on how to make a drinking gourd as well as links to other craft projects that gourds can be used for.

http://www.gardeningknowhow.com/garden-how-to/projects/crafts-with-gourds-how-to-make-water-canteens-from-dried-gourds.htm

Art Exercise

Have the students draw a picture of Peg Leg Joe, The Drinking Gourd, or the slaves running to freedom following the stars.

Astronomy Exercise

Since the Drinking Gourd is actually a seven star formation known as the Big Dipper, this lesson is an excellent way to foster an appreciation for Astronomy. Take your students outside at night and have them locate the Big Dipper, the Little Dipper and the North Star. Share with them that the North Star is also known as Polaris or the Pole Star and does actually point the way North.

Having Trouble Finding The Big Dipper?

How To Find The Big Dipper: http://lewisclark.cet.edu/student/activities/geography.html

Or Try: http://www.wikihow.com/Find-the-Big-Dipper

Have your students examine the night sky. Do they see any other star formations? What do they look like? Have them jot down what they see and then conduct research to discover the other star formations in the sky.

Spiritual Songs

Lesson Five

Lesson Five: Rebellion and Redemption

Objective: To gain a basic understanding of how the slaves used music to rebel against and reject slavery as well as explore unusual and little known stories of slave life.

Learning Outcomes

At the conclusion of this lesson students will:

- **Have a clear understanding of how music was used to fuel rebellion**
- **Articulate the concept of "freedom" and how it applies to us today**
- **Use critical thinking skills and explore journal writing**
- **Gain knowledge of unknown stories of slave rebellion and defiance**
- **Use vocabulary words that pertain to slavery, freedom and rebellion**

Lesson Five

Opening Learning Exercise:

Have the students write a journal entry and if willing share what they write about their concept of freedom. Questions to guide this exercise can include: what does it means to be free? What would life look like if that freedom was taken? The slaves often used music to express their desire for freedom and as a symbol of rebellion, what would the student use to express their desires? What would they use to express, encourage or discourage others to rebel? What actions would they be willing to take to obtain their freedom?

Have the students review the Oxford definition of freedom, and then write a second journal entry using the definition of freedom to further enhance or inform their thought process about the concept of freedom.

Oxford Definition of Freedom – Noun

The power or right to act, speak, or think as one wants without hindrance or restraint

Absence of subjection to foreign domination or despotic government

The state of not being imprisoned or enslaved

The state of being physically unrestricted and able to move easily

The state of not being subject to or affected by a particular undesirable thing

The power of self determination attributed to the will; the quality of being independent of fate or necessity

Unrestricted use of something, familiarity or openness in speech or behavior

*Teacher's Note: The following stories may contain subject matter not appropriate for younger learners. Please review them and decide which stories are a good match for the students in your learning community.

Lecture – Stories of Rebellion

Since slaves used music to express their faith, coordinate work, entertain themselves and express their emotions, the desire for freedom was also often expressed in the Negro Spiritual. One such song called, *Steal Away* describes how badly the slaves longed for freedom. Since the slaves did not "own" themselves and were the property of their Master, to escape was actually considered a crime of theft. If you were a runaway slave, you were in fact, "stealing" yourself! This song also implies that true freedom would only come through escape or death, and when death occurred, the slaves would truly be free based on the biblical promises they had learned and adopted as their own.

The lyrics to *Steal Away* are as follows:

Steal away, steal away, steal away to Jesus
Steal away, steal away home
I ain't got long to stay here

My Lord, He calls me
 He calls me by the thunder
The trumpet sounds within-a my soul
I ain't got long to stay here

Green trees are bending
Po' sinner stand a-trembling
The trumpet sounds within-a my soul
I ain't got long to stay here

An example of the song can be heard here: https://youtu.be/-O5hz5KnSdc

Lecture Two – The Ibo Drowning

The Ibo, also known as the Igbo or Ebo, are a cultural group based in Southern Nigeria on the Western Coast of Africa. They were often captured and sold into slavery forced to make the terrifying Middle Passage. Several versions of this particular story exist and some counter that it is in fact a legend or myth however, it is highly unlikely that some semblance of this story is not true.

A group of Ibo were sold into slavery and transported by ship to St. Simon's Island on Georgia's sea coast. Using the Dunbar River as their access to the shore the Ibo made a determined and drastic choice. The captured group's chief, so opposed to the thought of becoming a slave, in a spectacular act of defiance committed suicide by drowning himself in full view of everyone gathered.

Chanting and singing, "Water brought us, Water take us home!" the remainder of the tribe, chained together, acted as one and also proceeded to drown themselves in a stunning act of unity with their chief's actions.

Many Ibo were transported to this area of the country and many of their descents still live in this area today and are known as the Gullah people.

Growing Wings

Another prominent story tells of a group of slaves who want nothing more than to return to Africa. They visit the local conjurer man and ask him to make a way for them to return to their homeland. The man creates a powder, and pours it over the people who then sprout wings and fly back to Africa.

There are some researchers who believe that this story is based on true events, instead of the people growing wings, they participated in a suicide pact and jumped off a cliff.

In the Award Winning Children's book, *When the People Could Fly* all Africans can fly and have wings that were lost during The Middle Passage. But once the magic words were spoken, the ability to fly returns and the slaves are able to escape their cruel Masters.

Exercise for Younger Learners

Go to the library and check out or read the picture book, *When the People Could Fly* by Virginia Hamilton. This book is appropriate for readers from second to sixth grade. Discuss with your younger learners what freedom means and explore how the story impacts them. There are two versions of this book, so make sure the picture book is selected for younger readers.

Lecture Three
Margret Garner – Mother and Murderer

Born in 1834 on Maplewood Plantation in Kentucky, Margret Garner was a slave who was subjected to rape, abuse and giving birth to children some say were fathered by her plantation Master. Allowed to "marry" a slave from a nearby plantation, Robert Gardner, Margret, her husband and four children escaped across the Ohio River into Cincinnati on their way to Canada in 1856.

During their stop at a house on the Underground Railroad, they were overtaken by slave catchers determined to bring them back to Kentucky and enslave them again. Robert tried to protect his family by keeping the intruders at bay while Margret took the children into a back room. Garner then slit the throat of her two year old daughter, stabbed her three other children and herself, her youngest child dying instantly. Margret and her other children survived and were taken back into slavery.

Learning Exercise
Research Project – The Margaret Garner Trial

Margaret Garner was arrested and went on trial for the murder of her daughter. Although not covered in this curriculum, The Fugitive Slave Act made it possible for Garner to be arrested despite the fact that she was in a free state. Her trial was sensational and captured the attention of the mass media of its day. The core issue in the two-week trial pertained to the fact that Margaret was property and therefore not considered a "person" in the true sense of the word. Actual newspaper accounts can be found online and used as source material.

Questions to Consider During Research:

What actually happened to Margaret Garner?

What happened to Garner's children? Do you think Garner had a role in drowning her second daughter during a boating accident, as some suggest after being returned to the south?

How did the Fugitive Slave Act impact this case?

Was Margaret a person or in fact a piece of property?

Did Garner have the right to take the lives of her children?

Beloved by Toni Morrison

Award winning author, Toni Morrison was inspired by Garner's story to write the book, *Beloved*. A haunting tale, this story narrates the determination of a mother's will to control the lives and destiny of her family.

Caution: This book is a difficult read and contains aspects of the supernatural, as well as explicit language and strong sexual depictions. Educators are encouraged to read it themselves before assigning it to students to read to determine if it is in line with their academic and educational paradigm. Suggested reading level – mature, grades eleven and twelve. There is also a movie adaptation by Oprah Winfry that is equally disturbing and explicit.

Lecture Four
Amazing Grace – Story of Redemption

The song *Amazing Grace* is filled with hope, forgiveness and may be the most famous hymn of all time. The song was written by John Newton, an Englishman who had a history of drunkenness, desertion of the British Navy and slave trading.

Newton became a slave trader through the encouragement of his father who also dealt in the trade. During a trip on a slave ship, a terrifying storm arose and Newton perceived that the ship was going to sink. In desperation, he fell to his knees, called out to God to save him and the storm passed while cargo stored below shifted into position to close a hole in the ship's hull. Newton converted to Christianity, became a minister, and gave up the slave trade many years later. He went on to denounce his former activities encouraging abolitionist work in Europe through his writings and support of individuals such as William Wilberforce and writing the song, *Amazing Grace.*

Although Newton wrote the lyrics, originally as a poem, some scholars believe that it wasn't put to music until the 1800's and that the song uses as its melody a song entitled, *New Britannia.* Other scholars believe the melody was inspired by the West African Sorrow Songs that Newton may have heard coming up from the hold of the ships where he transported the slaves.

One thing we do know for certain, *Amazing Grace* can be played using only the black keys of the piano, the pentatonic scale, the scale associated with African music and the West African Sorrow Scale. Finally, *Amazing Grace* illustrates the beauty of hope restored, the power of God, forgiveness and the ability to turn from evil action and use your voice to impact the world for good.

View Amazing Grace being played on the piano:
Amazing Grace played on the Black Keys: https://youtu.be/VyCfKukzuYE

Learning Activity for Younger Learners:

Have the students sing the song *Amazing Grace* if they know the lyrics. If not, have them listen to the various renditions that can be found online. Aretha Franklin, Whitney Phillips, Judi Collins and Chris Tomlin all have a distinct delivery of the song that students can listen to and compare.

Have the students describe how the song makes them feel, what do they think the song is about and what does the song encourage them to believe.

Amazing Grace has a number of verses that are not well known or sung in church. Have the students locate in a hymnal, book, album or online, these verses and examine them. Have a discussion about what these verses mean, illustrate or imply.

If you use a faith based curriculum, use this story to draw connections between God's love, repentance, forgiveness and the power of redemption and doing good things.

Learning Exercise Work Sheet
Amazing Grace

Find five different renditions of the song *Amazing Grace*. Who is each rendition by? What type of music (pop, gospel, rock) does the artist you've selected primarily sing? Does the song fit in that genre of music?

Take a listen to each rendition, how are they similar, how are they different. Based on what you've already learned does the song sound like a Negro Spiritual? Why or why not?

How does the song *Amazing Grace* make you feel, what do you think the song is about and what does the song make you believe?

Amazing Grace has a number of verses that are not well known or sang in church. Locate a hymnal, book, album or look online to locate these verses and examine them. What do these other verses mean, illustrate or imply?

Learning Activity
Faith Based Curriculum Option
Amazing Grace **Lesson**

Using your Bible as a guide, how does the story of *Amazing Grace* draw connections between God's love, repentance, forgiveness and the power of redemption and doing good things?

Scripture References:
John 3 verse 16
1 John 1 verse 9
Isaiah 43 verse 25 and 26
Acts 3 Verse 19
2 Corinthians 5 Verse 17

Lesson Five Vocabulary Words and Terms

Instructions: These vocabulary words can be used in three ways.

1. Have students write down what they think the word means and then compare their definition with the dictionary's definition.
2. Conduct a spelling test or spelling bee or use other spelling games that help students identify and learn the proper spelling of these words.
3. Students can also be given an assignment to use each word in a sentence, essay, a poem or short story to assist in their development of language arts.

Beloved

Chant

Conjurer

Grace

Freedom

Pact

Rebellion

Redemption

Steal

Suicide

Wretch

Spiritual Songs

Lesson Six

Lesson Six: The End of the Civil War

Objective: To gain a basic understanding of how the Negro Spiritual made the transition into the 20th century, its impact on various historical events and the legacy the art form has left for the world.

Learning Outcomes

At the conclusion of this lesson students will:

- **Understand the impact the end of slavery had on the Negro Spiritual**
- **Discover Historical Black Colleges and Universities (HBCUs)**
- **Utilize research skills to access field recordings**
- **Gained knowledge on vocabulary words that pertain to the end of the Civil War and transformation of the Negro Spiritual to modern gospel music**

Lesson Six

Lecture – The Last Songs

As the Civil War came to a close the last Negro Spirituals were composed. These last songs focused on the themes of freedom and the celebration of the impending Northern victory. As the war came closer to its climax and conclusion, the North began to recruit African Americans to fight for the Union. Many male slaves left the plantations with no opposition because many of the Masters and their sons were away fighting the war. Many simply ran away to join the Union army and these slaves were often called, Contraband.

African Americans who joined the army were part of what was known as "all colored" divisions or regiments. Negro Spirituals were often sung in the camps of these African American soldiers. They sang songs in tribute to John Brown, a white man who led a revolt in Harper's Ferry, VA to bring about an end of slavery.

Learning Exercise

Have the students conduct research about John Brown and the rebellion that he led. Discuss his rebellion and its impact on slavery, slaves and their Masters. Many plantation owners saw John Brown as a traitor and murderer; many African Americans saw him as a hero. Based on the research found, discuss with the students if they think John Brown was a hero, traitor, or both. Ask the students to justify their reasoning with historical support and concrete answers.

Examine the lyrics of the song, *John Brown's Body*. Discuss why the soldiers would have sung such lyrics.

Learning Exercise Worksheet
Song Lyrics - *John Brown's Body*

John Brown's body lies a-mouldering in the grave,
John Brown's body lies a-mouldering in the grave,
But his soul goes marching on.

Chorus
Glory, glory, hallelujah,
Glory, glory, hallelujah,
His soul goes marching on.

He's gone to be a soldier in the Army of the Lord,
He's gone to be a soldier in the Army of the Lord,
His soul goes marching on.

John Brown's knapsack is strapped upon his back,
John Brown's knapsack is strapped upon his back,
His soul goes marching on.

John Brown died that the slaves might be free,
John Brown died that the slaves might be free,
His soul goes marching on.

The stars above in Heaven now are looking kindly down,
The stars above in Heaven now are looking kindly down,
His soul goes marching on.

Discussion Notes:

Learning Exercises

Glory

To view a depiction of the African American soldiers singing in the war camps, have the students view a clip from the movie, *Glory* starring Denzel Washington and Morgan Freeman. https://youtu.be/tzUUFwbPaE4

Glory would also be an excellent movie to have older learners watch to learn more about African Americans in the Civil War and their roles in actual battles.

For The South

There were African Americans who fought in the Confederate army. Have the students spend time doing research on these regiments and discussing possible reason African Americans may have served in such divisions.

Lecture Two – Gonna Lay Down My Burdens

Another Negro Spiritual sung during the war was, *Gonna Lay Down My Burdens*. This song specifically describes what the slaves would do once the war was finally over and they were free. They were ready to lay down all of their troubles and embrace freedom, while looking forward with great eagerness to the end of the war. *Gonna Lay Down My Burdens*, may be one of the last Negro Spirituals to be composed. The lyrics are listed below. This is a fun song to sing as it is upbeat and full of hope. Have the students search online for various versions of the song. The Negro Spiritual has impacted singers from all genres, and this song was sung by many great artists. One of the most popular renditions was even sung by Elvis Presley!

Gonna Lay Down My Burdens

I'm gonna lay down my burden, down by the riverside
Down by the riverside, down by the riverside
I'm gonna lay down my burden, down by the riverside
Down by the riverside, down by the riverside
Ain't gonna study war no more
Ain't gonna study war no more, I ain't gonna study war no more

Well, I'm a lay down my sword and shield
Down by the riverside, down by the riverside
Down by the riverside
Ain't gonna study war no more!

Lecture Two – A Devastating Loss

When the Civil War came to an end in 1865, slavery was abolished by the 13th Amendment of the Constitution and the Negro Spiritual almost faded away, lost into history. Large numbers of the newly freed slave population left the plantations to seek family members, escape racism or find better opportunities in the Northern states.

African Americans began to develop their own churches while others joined and participated in traditional church organizations, both were more formal in style and worship approaches. In many instances, hymns became routine and the Call and Response Songs, and more rousing spirituals were not sung at all. Many African Americans no longer wanted to sing those "old songs" as they reminded them of their days on the plantations and of sadness and slavery.

Remember!

Slaves could not read or write, and this was before the time of recording studios and MP3s, so many of these songs were never recorded or written down. Slaves learned the Spirituals because they were taught them by other slaves, the songs were passed down from generation to generation or from plantation to plantation. Since the songs were not written down, there is no way to really know how many of these songs existed, or what the exact words, melodies or arrangements were. What we have today is a compilation of music that has been collected, recreated and rearranged over the last one hundred and fifty years.

Many scholars think that hundreds of songs may have been lost during this time of transition. And since the songs were not being sung, they were almost forgotten about. The Negro Spiritual almost became extinct. Then two things happened to save the Negro Spiritual and bring it back to the artistic forefront.

Lecture Three – Fisk University

Fisk University was founded in 1866 by the American Missionary Association and General Clinton Fisk with the goal of educating former slaves and their children. Located in Nashville, TN, Fisk often struggled to find financial donors since the University's mission centered on giving African American's a liberal arts education instead of a vocational one. Most people did not believe that African Americans should be taught the Arts, Sciences and Humanities. They favored teaching them skills such as sewing, farming and carpentry. After being open a short time, the University was facing bankruptcy and the possibility of closing forever.

In an effort to save the school, George L. White, a music teacher and school treasurer decided to form a choir and take them on a musical tour. The tour was a failure at first, not many people wanted to hear the African American students singing Arias and Classical Music. At an event in Oberlin, Ohio the choir decided to add several of the songs their parents and grandparents sang, the Negro Spirituals. Their renditions of these songs were received with overwhelming support and success. The choir rose over $1,500.00 at that event, a sum unheard of at that time.

The choir became so renown, that they acquired a booking agent and toured the country singing in churches and venues such as Plymouth Church in Brooklyn, led by famed abolitionist Pastor Henry Ward Beecher, father of Harriet Beecher Stowe who wrote the American classic on slavery, *Uncle Tom's Cabin*. The choir rose over $20,000.00 on their first tour and continued to raise funds to keep the university running.

The choir traveled internationally, doing a command performance for Queen Victoria in Great Britain. The choir is also responsible for turning the Negro Spiritual into classically performed concert songs where they married the emotion and lyrics with an operatic style of performance.

That choir, which started so many years ago and saved Fisk University from closing, is still in existence today. They are called The Fisk Jubilee Singers, and they have sung all over the world, have had documentaries made about them and have also recorded many CDs.

Since the newly freed slaves could not read or write, and they were not allowed to be educated with their white peers, many schools and colleges were founded that specifically addressed the needs of African Americans. Some were vocational schools, focusing more on subjects such as agriculture and domestic sciences. But many were liberal arts institutions focusing on what many people call a classical education, covering areas such as music, law, history and languages. Some specifically focused on teaching and preparing students for religious service.

Today over 100 of these schools survive and many are quite prestigious with a long history of academic excellence and fine tradition. These colleges and universities include schools such as: Howard University in Washington, DC, Spellman College for Women in Atlanta, GA and Hampton University in Hampton, VA. Today, these schools are called, HBCU's (Historically Black Colleges and Universities) and although they now enroll students from every nation, culture and race, they are primarily attended by African American students. Famous African Americans such as: Martin Luther King, Jr., Alice Walker, Common, Oprah Winfry, Tarji P. Hairston, Yolanda Adams and Thurgood Marshall all attended an HBCU.

Learning Exercise – History of Historically Black Colleges and Universities

Have the students conduct research on Historically Black Colleges and Universities. Possible research topics can include:

Have the students search online, visit the library, look up information on The United Negro College Fund or The Journal of Blacks in Higher Education to develop a list of HBCUs. Which school was founded first and where? What was the mission of that institution? Is that mission still needed today? Why or why not? Does that school still exist?

Have the students visit the school's web pages and learn more about some of the HBCUs they discover.

Have the students research the struggles that HBCU's face in the 21st century and examine the current graduation and retention rates. What patterns exist? How can these problems be solved?

Have the students watch an episode of *A Different World*, this 1990's comedy sitcom focuses on life at a fictional historically black college.

Find an HBCU near your location and go for a tour to learn about the rich history and traditions that exist there.

Some HBCU's include: Howard University, Wilberforce University, Central State, Fisk University, Tuskegee University, Norfolk State, Hampton University, Spelman College, Bethune Cookman, Edward Waters, and Grambling State.

Lecture Four – Government Documentation

As the 19th century came to a close and many of the men who fought in the Civil War were dying, the United States Government thought that the war stories and experiences of the Confederate Soldiers from the South should be recorded and preserved. Researchers were sent to various Southern states to interview the last of the Confederates. Some of these veterans still lived on the plantations they were born and raised on and there were still African Americans living there. Some working the land for very little pay, in a system known as sharecropping and some living there because they were elderly and had lived on the land all of their lives.

While the interviews were being conducted, many researchers also thought that recording the songs and experiences of the former slaves was just as important to preserve. They recorded these stories, as well as many of the Negro Spirituals we know and sing today and have become known as the *Civil War Field Recordings*. They are a vast collection of different articles, recordings, books and music that is stored within the Library of Congress and some of this information can be reviewed on line.

Thomas Dorsey – The Father of Modern Gospel Music

The Negro Spiritual has truly impacted all forms and types of music that we know and love today. Its influence can be seen greatly in the work of W.C. Handy, the son of a pastor who is known as The Father of The Blues. The Blues, another African American birthed art form consists of songs that center on the troubles of life, such as poverty, violence, and broken hearts. Handy often used elements of spiritual music in his compositions.

Buddy Bolden, another great African American artist is considered the Father of Jazz music, another distinctly American musical art form that also sprang from the Blues and the Negro Spiritual. As discussed in an earlier lesson, this influence extends to hip hop, cheerleading and R and B music.

The most direct descendent of the Negro Spiritual is however, modern Gospel Music, often called Black Gospel Music. Today's popular artists such as: Tye Tribett, Mary Mary, Kirk Franklin and Tasha Cobb all sing music that was birthed from this powerful historical art form.

Gospel Music holds Thomas Dorsey as its founder. Originally a Blues and Jazz artist, Dorsey traveled the country playing in night clubs and bars while also maintaining his ties to the music of the church. During the 1930's, while Dorsey was touring, he was informed that his wife, Nettie and new baby had died tragically. Overcome by grief, Dorsey penned one of the greatest hymns of all time, *Precious Lord*. At first, Dorsey's new hymn was condemned by the church, many felt the song resembled the Blues and was too soulful to be sung in worship services. But over time these perceptions changed and the modern genre of Gospel Music was born.

The Negro Spiritual is a distinctly American art form, music sung and created by a people who were instrumental in building this nation. We should never forget their struggle, their loss or the terror that was and in some parts of the world still is – slavery. But we should also joyfully sing their songs no matter what we look like, because these are songs of hope, of faith and of freedom – and everyone deserves that.

Music/Audio Videos

Fisk Jubilee Singers – 1909 - https://youtu.be/GUvBGZnL9rE

Fisk Jubilee Singers – Today - https://youtu.be/sLU70RBqxJE

Thomas Dorsey – Precious Lord Take My Hand - https://youtu.be/7xn8RpQyX4M

Mary Mary – Shackles - https://youtu.be/V7eZD3TKn_M

Lesson Six Vocabulary Words and Terms

Instructions: These vocabulary words can be used in three ways.

1. Have students write down what they think the word means and then compare their definition with the dictionary's definition.
2. Conduct a spelling test or spelling bee or use other spelling games that help students identify and learn the proper spelling of these words.
3. Students can also be given an assignment to use each word in a sentence, essay, a poem or short story to assist in their development of language arts.

Amendment

Bankruptcy

Carpentry

Classical

Confederate

Compilation

Constitution

Donors

Extinct

Faded

Forefront

Formal

Devastating

Humanities

Jubilee

Liberal Arts

Morph

Moulder (Sometimes spelled Molder)

Rousing

Traitor

Veterans

Vocational

Lesson Six: Quick Quiz

1. Who was John Brown, and what did he do?

2. Name a song sung by the African American soldiers during the Civil War. Describe what that song portrays.

3. Why were there no new Negro Spirituals created after the Civil War?

4. Who were the Fisk Jubilee Singers and how did they help save the Negro Spiritual?

5. What types of music has the Negro Spiritual influenced?

Resources

For

Spiritual Songs Curriculum

True or False Spiritual Songs Final Exam

Negro Spirituals were first called yard songs _____

In Africa, they used the drum to send messages _____

The Howard Singers helped save the Negro Spiritual _____

When *The People Could Fly* may have been based on real events _____

Harriet Tubman was the inspiration for Go Down Moses _____

Amazing Grace was written by Thomas Newtown _____

The Underground Railroad was an actual train that ran on a track _____

Negro Spirituals can be played using only the black piano keys _____

Lay Down My Burdens was written before 1865 _____

This Little Light of Mine is a "Call and Response" Song _____

Daniel Little is "The Father of Modern Gospel Music _____

The origin of Negro Spirituals is West African Sorrow Songs _____

Spiritual Songs Curriculum
Dr. Naima Johnston Bush © 2017

True and False Teacher Key

Negro Spirituals were first called yard songs	FALSE
In Africa they used the drum to send messages	TRUE
The Howard Singers helped save the Negro spiritual	FALSE
When *The People Could Fly* may have been based on real events	TRUE
Harriet Tubman was the inspiration for Go Down Moses	TRUE
Amazing Grace was written by Thomas Newtown	FALSE
The Underground Railroad was an actual train that ran on a track	FALSE
Negro Spirituals can be played using only the black piano keys	TRUE
Gonna Lay Down My Burdens was written before 1865	TRUE
This Little Light of Mine is a "Call and Response" Song	TRUE
Daniel Little was "The Father of Modern Gospel Music	FALSE
The origin of Negro Spirituals are West African Sorrow Songs	TRUE

The Spiritual Songs Word Search

```
Q E P U W U D M Y Y G W D Z U X I I F P Y H E I V
K J D M F H M R A F P I K R M T L N D A Y H J O J
L G V L Z Q T K K W Y S T H U D K T E F M S K B V
K T X L K Z U L U F I G H K W M H A L O S M A O B
Z V U E X U V Q M F Z O Z Z R G S O O L I E Y N C
M V P W C C I I B Y C S Z W L J K J F Q Z A P S A
I N P H X V L O Y W T P C I O W E F Y V J A G J E
J Q B F I C M E Y J D E Q Y L V A C W N Z L R V F
L C E F E C G O A F I L A O S I H W P Y D C R S Z
M W G F A F S A T Z P W R G W A I L E B S M E B B
D C G V I R G O J H P S E P Y G J Z Z Y Z I I U Z
Z J K M H D M B R L E C B R M H C Q I Z T R O R P
J O F V X N O S W R R E O J O W P X T E A A D D
A I Q U X P N D U B O T L P V O O H I O R B F E E
U P N E H G A M N R L W L E H O N D W G K O R N M
G X R G I O U V S B U Q I R S Q M F A V O L I S T
L C E U R U Y G R C Y C O T Y S M U R O P I C X W
G N P L J D I O Y X M G N Y P I C Y G J K T A J G
G X I I L S D U M X J X V K C O C T X T Q I O K E
A A Q H H H S R M X A V H Q M N E I S C I O A K G
R U X C T O P D D U E B X M X F F B V H J N U Z C
Q M I F A M T P T Z C P U V H X U C H I Z G W D C
X K H Z X R V N Y V H Z E P C J M Q C A L W B J X
M X E N S L A V E R Y L G N P X K C P H P Y B M D
K U J Y F V C L H J X L X Q S B Y U Z E A T A A W
```

Abolition, Africa, Burdens, Civil, Dipper, Ditties, Drums, Fisk, Gospel, Gourd, Kum By Ya, Motherless, Ohio, Property, Railroad, Rebellion, Slavery, Sorrow, War

```
Q E P U W U D M Y   Y G W D Z U X I I   F P Y H E I V
K J D M F H M R A F P I K R M T L N   D A Y H J O J
L G V L Z Q T K K W Y S T H U D K T   E F M S K B V
K T X L K Z U L U F I G H K W M H A L O S M A O B
Z V U E X U V Q M F Z O Z Z R G S O O L I E Y N C
M V P W C C I I B Y C S Z W L J K J   F Q Z A P S A
I N P H X V L O Y W T P C I O W E F   Y V J A G J E
J Q B F I C M E Y J D E Q Y L V A C   W N Z L R V F
L C E F E C G O A F I L A O S I H W   P Y D       Z
M W G F A F S A T Z P W R G W A I L E B S       Z B
D C G V I R G O J H P S E     G J Z Z Y Z       Z
Z J K M H D M B R L E C B     H C Q I Z T       P
J O F V X N O S W R R E     O W P X T E       D
A I Q U X P N D U B O T L   O O H I O R       E
U P N E H G A M N R L W L   O N D W G K       M
G X R G I O U V S B U Q I   Q M F A V O       T
L C E U R U Y G R C Y C O   S M U R O P       W
G N P L J D I O Y X M G N   I C Y G J K       G
G X I I L S D U M X J X V K C O C T X T Q I O K E
A A Q H H H S R M X A V H Q M N E I S C I O A K G
R U X C T O P D D U E B X M X F F B V H J N U Z C
Q M I F A M T P T Z C P U V H X U C H I Z G W D C
X K H Z X R V N Y V H Z E P C J M Q C A L W B J X
M X E N S L A V E R Y L G N P X K C P H P Y B M D
K U J Y F V C L H J X L X Q S B Y U Z E A T A A W
```

Spiritual Songs Bible Study

Faith Builder: If the educational community is faith based in nature, have the students study the book of Exodus in the Old Testament as well as the life of Moses. You can use the questions listed below as a starting off point or you can purchase an independent Bible study to use in conjunction with this study.

What similarities do you see between the story of the Israelites and the Africans?

Moses was originally supposed to be a slave but the Lord had a different idea. What was God's plan for Moses?

Harriet Tubman is known as the Black Moses. What are the differences and similarities between Harriet Tubman and Moses?

How did the Lord use Moses to free the slaves?

What Scriptures outline the treatment of slaves?

According to the Bible what is the year of Jubilee? If Slave Owners followed The Bible how would this have impacted the institution of slavery?

Other Resources

The Field Recordings – The American Folk Life Center at The Library of Congress
https://www.loc.gov/folklife/guides/Spirituals.html

Picture Books

All Night, All Day, A Child's First Book of African American Spirituals by Ashley Bryan

He's Got The Whole World In His Hands by Kadir Nelson

Let it Shine by Ashley Bryan

Like a Bird: The Art of the American Slave Song by Cynthia Grady and Michele Wood

Follow the Drinking Gourd by Jeanette Winter

Freedom Songs: A Tale of the Underground Railroad by Trina Robbins

Many Thousands Gone by Virginia Hamilton

Show Way by Jacqueline Woodson

Sweet Clara and the Freedom Quilt by Deborah Hopkinson

Older Readers

Elijah of Buxton by Christopher Paul Curtis

Dark Midnight When I Rise, The Story of the Jubilee Singers by Andrew Ward

Incidents in the Life of a Slave Girl by Harriet Jacobs

No Man Cannot Hinder Me by Velma Maia Thomas

No More! Stories and Songs of Slave Resistance by Doreen Rappaport

Psalms Hymns and Spiritual Songs, Reflections on the Negro Spiritual by Dr. Naima Johnston Bush

Passenger on the Pearl: The True Story of Emily Edmonson's Flight from Slavery by Winifred Conkling

Negro Slave Songs in the United States by Miles Mark Fisher

Slave Songs of the United States by William Francis and Charles Ware

Stolen Into Slavery: The True Story of Solomon Northup, Free Black Man by Judith Bloom Fradin and Denis Brindell Fradin

The People Could Fly by Virginia Hamilton (Not the picture book)

Uncle Tom's Cabin by Harriet Beecher Stowe

Movies (Most of these movies are not appropriate for younger learners. The teacher should watch them before sharing them with students.)

A Woman Called Moses – Retelling of the life of Harriet Tubman.

Amazing Grace – Based on the true story of William Wilberforce and the abolitionist movement in Great Britain.

Amistad – Based on the true story of a slave ship rebellion.

Belle – Based on the true story of a Black heiress in England during the 1700's.

Jubilee Singers, Sacrifice and Glory – PBS, The American Experience

Night John – Fictional account of a young slave girl who learns to read and write, excellent for younger learners.

Roots – Based on the true story of Alex Hayley's family, starting in Africa to the end of the civil war. The original mini series with LaVar Burton is best.

The Underground Railroad – The William Still Story, PBS, The American Experience

Music

Amazing Grace – Aretha Franklin

Emmanuel, An African Christmas – The African Children's Choir

Gospel Music Hall of Fame Series: The Fisk Jubilee Singers

Let My People Go, Negro Spirituals, Roots Collection Volume 9

Negro Spirituals – Mahailia Jackson

Spirituals – Marian Anderson

These books, movies and music can all be purchased online at: The Wisdom Store, Powered by Amazon: http://www.winsor413.com/wisdom-book-store

Videos

Prison Songs/ Call and Response
Lighting Long John
https://youtu.be/4G5KtQynWvc

Opera Greats – Kathleen Battle and Jessye Norman Sing Spirituals
Full Concert
https://youtu.be/bK0X9J_pX8w

The Story of Gospel Music, Power in the Voice
Full Documentary
https://youtu.be/iC0rg0LywHw

WC Handy – Father of the Blues
https://youtu.be/EkOcO5HXbk8

Make Your Own Drum

Would you like to make your own Djembe drum? This website offers easy, clear and concise instructions on how to create your own drum. The supplies needed are easy to obtain and are things most of us already have around the house.

http://artsmarts4kids.blogspot.com/2008/10/create-your-own-african-djembe-drum.html

Bid Em' In

This short cartoon video depicts how slaves were sold on the auction block in the 1800's. The cartoon is set to a song written by Oscar Brown, Jr. who was a renowned jazz, soul and blues artist as well as a playwright and social activist. This video is recommended for ages ten years and older.

The video can be seen here: https://youtu.be/Tu3j7rPscpY

Discussion Questions Based on *Bid Em' In*

Research the life of Oscar Brown, Jr. why do you think he wrote this song?

What strikes you as interesting about the song *Bid Em' In*?

Search for the lyrics of *Bid Em' In* online, what lines of the song stand out to you? Why?

Circle any words from the lyrics you don't know the meaning of and define them. Does that change what you think about the song?

How does the song make you feel?

The Dahomey Queens

Dahomey was a kingdom in West Africa that was renamed Benin in 1975. The kingdom's most famous and fiercest warriors were women, led by women generals who were charged with protecting the nation, expanding the kingdom's boarders and protecting the royal family. These female troops were termed Amazons and were active for over 200 years from 1600 – 1900.

The auctioneer calls the African woman he's selling a "Dahomey Queen."

Write a one page essay on the Dahomey using research gathered from the internet. Here are some questions to help guide your essay writing.

What were the women warriors like? What interesting facts have you learned about the Dahomey? Who finally conquered the Dahomey? Why do you think the auctioneer used the term Dahomey Queen when refereeing to the African woman he was selling in the video? What is the current status of the Dahomey kingdom today?

Websites to Help Guide Your Research

http://www.smithsonianmag.com/history/dahomeys-women-warriors-88286072/?no-ist

Spiritual Songs Curriculum
By Dr. Naima Johnston Bush
© 2017 7thirtyseven Logos Publishing

Notes:

Dr. Naima Tonya Johnston Bush

A dynamic educator, author and artist, Dr. Naima Johnston Bush uses her artistic gifts to educate, entertain and encourage audiences across the nation. The founder of Winsor Educational Services, Dr. Johnston Bush travels performing, speaking and teaching seminars to colleges, businesses, churches, religious groups, musical venues, and other social and civic organizations.

Naima has had the chance to create dynamic and interactive programs, concerts and workshops that delight, challenge and engage her participants gaining numerous fans acquired from teaching, speaking and performing in states such as Florida, Georgia, Kentucky, Kansas, Illinois, Wisconsin, New York, Ohio, Maryland, Connecticut, Missouri, Indiana and Tennessee. Naima is the author of the booklet: *5 Things I Wish Someone Would Have Told Me My Freshman Year*, as well as the book, *Go With What You Got, A Dream Development Manual* and was recently published in the *Sistah Faith Anthology* edited by Essence best selling author Marilynn Griffith and published by Simon and Shuster. Naima released her book, *Confessions of a Big Girl, Reflections on Fat, Faith and Femininity* to critical acclaim and recently released, *Psalms, Hymns and Spiritual Songs; Reflections on the Negro Spiritual.*

Originally from New York City, Naima holds a BA in Sociology and Women's Studies from Ohio Wesleyan University and an MA in Higher Education Administration from The Ohio State University. A former fulltime educator on the college level, Naima completed her PhD in Educational Foundations at The Ohio State University. Her educational expertise includes: Curriculum Development, Qualitative Research Methodology, Leadership, Educational Diversity and Inclusion. Naima has served as a former Director of Residence Life and Associate Director of Student Life and continues her educational work as a consultant, keynote speaker, and trainer for various organizations, businesses, colleges and universities.

Winsor Consulting Services provides personal seminars, keynote speeches and creative programs that center on issues such as: diversity, life coaching, self esteem, health and wellness, student success, faith and spirituality, student leadership and development, Greek Affairs, and personal and professional development. Past clients include: Bluffton College, Wittenberg University, McMurry College, Illinois College, Sinclair Community College, University of Dayton, Neuman College and Ohio Wesleyan University.

Naima is a member of: ASCAP, Delta Sigma Theta Sorority, Inc. the largest African American women's organization in the world and a former Alumni Board Member of Ohio Wesleyan University. Naima makes her home with her husband Pastor Jon Bush and their two dogs Bianca Wee Wee Monster and Bucho the Moocher.